Introduction
to
Freemasonry
(Entered Apprentice)
(Volume 1)

by

Carl H. Claudy

ISBN: 9781631829697

Introduction to Freemasonry

Printed January, 2014

Published and Distributed By:

Lushena Books
607 Country Club Drive, Unit E
Bensenville, IL 60106
www.lushenabks.com

ISBN: 9781631829697

Printed in the United States of America

INTRODUCTION TO FREEMASONRY

ENTERED APPRENTICE

At your leisure hours, that you may improve in Masonic knowledge, you are to converse with well-informed brethren, who will always be as ready to give, as you will be ready to receive, instruction.

These words from the Charge to an Entered Apprentice set forth the purpose of the three little books, of which this is the first: to give to the initiate, in his leisure hours, some "instruction" and information about the Fraternity not wholly imparted in the ceremonies of initiation.

These volumes are intended as simple introductions to the study of the Ancient Craft; the interested Freemason will look further, for other and longer books; the uninterested will not, perhaps, read all of these! Had completeness been the aim, these little books might have become forbiddingly large.

No more has been attempted than to give some Masonic light on some of the history, jurisprudence, symbols, customs, and landmarks of the Order, by the rays of which any initiate may readily find his way down the path of Masonic learning which leads to the gate of truth.

These books are far more gateways than guides to the foreign country of Freemasonry. However elemental they may be to the Masonic student, if their very simplicity leads those Entered Apprentices, Fellowcrafts, and newly raised Master Masons for whom they were written to seek more Masonic light, their purpose will have been served and their preparation well worth the time and effort spent upon them.

DEFINITION

Freemasonry is a system of morality, veiled in allegory, and illustrated by symbols.

This definition of the Ancient Craft means much more to the well-informed Freemason than to the initiate, to whom it can convey but little. Naturally he wants to know "Why *Freemasonry?* Why is it veiled? Why illustrated with symbols?"

Masons are "Free and Accepted" for reasons which are to be found in the early history of Freemasonry.

EARLY HISTORY

Many of Freemasonry's symbols and teachings go back to the very childhood of the race. Through these a direct relationship may be traced, in mind and heart and ideal, if not in written document, to such diverse ages and places as China four thousand years ago, the priesthood of ancient Egypt, and the Jews of the Captivity. But for purposes of understanding the genesis of the word "free" as coupled with "Mason," it will suffice to begin with the Roman *Collegia*: orders or associations of men engaged in similar pursuits. Doubtless their formation was caused by the universal desire for fellowship and association, particularly strong in Rome, in which the individual was so largely submerged for the good of the empire, as well as by economic necessity, just as labor unions are formed to-day.

These *Collegia* speedily became so prominent and powerful that Roman emperors attempted to abolish the right of free association. In spite of edicts and persecutions, some of the *Collegia* continued to exist.

The Colleges of Architects, however, were sanctioned for a time even after others were forbidden. They were too valuable to the state to be abolished or made to work and meet in secret. They were not at this time *called* Freemasons, but they were *free*—and it is the fact and not the name which is here important. Without architects and builders Rome could not expand, so the Colleges of Architects were permitted to regulate their own affairs and work under their own constitutions, free of the restrictions which were intended to destroy other *Collegia*.

Then, as now, *three* were necessary to form a College (no Masonic lodge can meet with less than three); the College had a *Magister* or Master, and two Wardens. There were three orders or degrees in the College which, to a large extent, used emblems which are a part of Freemasonry. Roman sarcophagi show carvings of a square, compasses, plumb, level, and sometimes columns.

Of the ceremonies of the *Collegia* we know little or nothing. Of their work we know much, and of their history, enough to trace their decline and fall. The Emperor Diocletian attempted to destroy the new religion, Christianity, which threatened so much which seemed to the Romans to make Rome, Rome. Many members of the Colleges of Architects were Christians. Since these associations had taught and believed in brotherhood, when there came a Carpenter who taught brotherhood because of a common Father, the members of the Colleges of Architects took His doctrine, so strangely familiar, for their own.

Persecution, vengeance, cruelty followed; this is not the place to go into the story of the four Masons and the apprentice who were tortured to death, only to become the four crowned martyrs and patron saints of later builders and the Masons of the Middle Ages. Suffice it that the Colleges of Architects were broken up and fled from Rome.

Comes a gap which is not yet bridged. Between the downfall of Rome and the rise of Gothic architecture we know little of what happened to the builders' *Collegia*. It is here that we come to the fascinating story of the Comacines. Some of the expelled builders found refuge on the island of Comacina in Lake Como and, through generation after generation, kept alive the traditions and secrets of their art until such time as the world was again ready for the Master Builders. All this is most interestingly set forth in several books, best known of which is Leader Scott's *Cathedral Builders; The Story of a Great Masonic Guild.* The author says that the Comacine Masters "were the link between the classic *Collegia* and all other art and trade guilds of the Middle Ages. They were Freemasons because they were builders of a privileged class, absolved from taxes and servitude, and free to travel about in times of feudal bondage."

ENTERED APPRENTICE

During the Middle Ages and the rise of Gothic architecture we find two distinct classes of Masons; the Guild Masons, who, like the Guild carpenters or weavers or merchants, were local in character and strictly regulated by law, and the Freemasons, who traveled about from city to city as their services were needed to design and erect those marvelous churches and cathedrals which stand to-day inimitable in beauty. It may not be affirmed as a proved fact that the Freemasons of the Middle Ages were the direct descendants through the Comacine Masters of the Colleges of Architects of Rome, but there is too much evidence of a similar structure, ideal, and purpose, and too many similarities of symbol, tool, and custom, to dismiss the idea merely because we have no written record covering the period between the expulsion from Rome and the beginning of the cathedral-building age.

However this may be, the operative builders and designers of the cathedrals of Europe were an older Order than the Guild Masons; it is from these Freemasons—free of the Guild and free of the local laws —that the Freemasonry of to-day has come. Incidentally, it may be noted that the historian Findel finds that the name Freemason appears as early as 1212, and the name occurs in 1375 in the history of the Company of Masons of the City of London.

The history of the Freemasons through the cathedral-building ages up to the Reformation and the gradual decline of the building art needs volumes where here are but pages. But it must be emphasized that the Freemasons were far more than architects and builders; they were artists, the leaders, the teachers, the mathematicians and the poets of their time. In their lodges Speculative Masonry grew side by side with their operative art. They were jealous of their Order and strict in their acceptance of Apprentices; strict in admitting Apprentices to be Fellows of the Craft, requiring seven years of labor of an Apprentice before he might make his "Master's Piece" to submit to the Master and Wardens of his lodge, when, haply, he might become a Fellow and receive "the Mason Word."

In an age when learning was difficult to get and association with the educated hardly to be had outside of the church, it was but natural that thoughtful and scholarly men should desire membership among the Freemasons. Such men, however, would not want to practice operative masonry, or serve a seven years' apprenticeship. Therefore a place was made for them by taking them in as *accepted* Masons; that is, accepted as members having something to offer and desiring to receive something from the lodge, but distinguished from the operative Freemasons by the title *accepted*.

It is not possible to say when this practice began. The Regius Poem,[1] the oldest document of Free-

---

[1] Halliwell Manuscript, the oldest of the written Constitutions, transcribed in 1390, probably from an earlier version. Called Halliwell because first published in 1840 by James O. Halliwell, who first discovered its Masonic character. Prior to that date it was catalogued in the Royal Library as *A Poem of Moral Duties*. Called the Regius Poem partly because it formed part of Henry VIII's Royal Library and partly because it is the first and therefore the kingly or royal document of the Craft.

masonry (1390), speaks of Prince Edward (Tenth Century) as:

Of speculatyfe he was a master.

Desiring to become architects and builders, ecclesiasts joined the order. Lovers of liberty were naturally attracted to a fellowship in which members enjoyed unusual freedom.

Through the years, particularly those which saw the decline of great building and the coming of the Reformation, more and more became the Accepted Masons and less and less the operative building Freemasons. Of forty-nine names on the roll of the Lodge of Aberdeen in the year 1670, thirty-nine were those of Accepted Masons.

Hence our title—Free and Accepted Masons, abbreviated F. & A. M. There are variations in certain jurisdictions,[1] such as F. and A. M. (Free and Accepted Masons), A. F. & A. M. (Ancient Free and Accepted Masons), etc., the origin of which the student may find in the history of Freemasonry of the Grand Lodge era. (*See* Page 121, footnote)

---

[1] Jurisdiction: the territory and the Craft in it over which a Grand Lodge is sovereign. In the United States are forty-nine; one for each state and the District of Columbia. Used as a brevity; thus, the Masonic jurisdiction of New Jersey means "all the Masonry, lodges, Masons in the State of New Jersey over which rules the Grand Lodge of the Most Ancient and Honorable Society of Free and Accepted Masons for the State of New Jersey."

The word also means the territorial boundaries to which the right of a lodge to accept petitions extends.

INTRODUCTION TO FREEMASONRY

ALLEGORY AND SYMBOLS

Freemasonry is "veiled in allegory and illustrated by symbols" because these are the surest ways by which moral and ethical truths may be taught. It is not only with the brain and the mind that the initiate must take in Freemasonry but also with the heart.

Mind speaks to mind with spoken or written words. Heart speaks to heart with words which cannot be written or spoken. Those words are symbols; words which mean little to the indifferent, much to the understanding.

The body has its five senses through which the mind may learn; the mind has also imagination. That imagination may see farther than eyes and hear sounds fainter than may be caught by ears. To the imagination symbols become plain as printed words to the eye. Nothing else will do; no words can be as effective (unless they are themselves symbols); no teachings expressed in language are as easily learned by the mind as those which come *via* the symbol through the imagination.

Take from Freemasonry its symbols and but the husk remains, the kernel is gone. He who hears but the words of Freemasonry misses their meaning entirely.

THE LODGE

During the ceremonies of initiation the Entered Apprentice is informed what a lodge is. In other than the words of the ritual a Masonic lodge is a body of Masons warranted or chartered as such by its

Grand Lodge and possessing the three Great Lights in Masonry.

The lodge usually [1] comes into being when a certain number of brethren petition the Grand Master, who, if it is his pleasure, issues a dispensation which forms these brethren into a provisional lodge, or a lodge under dispensation, familiarly known as U. D. The powers of the U. D. lodge are strictly limited; it is not yet a "regularly constituted lodge" but an inchoate sort of organization, a fledgling in the nest. Not until the Grand Lodge has authorized the issuance of the warrant does it assume the status of a "regular" lodge, and not then until it is consecrated, dedicated, and constituted by the Grand Master and his officers, or those he delegates for the ceremony. The warrant of the new lodge names its first Worshipful Master, Senior Warden, and Junior Warden, who hold office until their successors are duly elected and installed.

Lodge officers are either elected or appointed. In some lodges in some jurisdictions all officers in the "line" are elected. In others only the Master, Senior and Junior Wardens, Secretary and Treasurer are elected, the others being appointed.

The term of office is one year, but nothing prevents reëlection of a Master or Wardens. Indeed, Secretaries and Treasurers generally serve as long as they

---

[1] The oldest lodges in a Grand Lodge existed prior to its formation and came into being from a warrant or charter from some other Grand Lodge, or, in some few instances of very old lodges, merely by brethren getting together and holding a lodge under "immemorial custom." Thus, Fredericksburg Lodge of Virginia, in which Washington received his degrees, had no warrant until several years after its formation.

are willing; a lodge almost invariably reëlects the same incumbents year after year to these places. These officers become the connecting links between different administrations, which practice makes for stability and smooth running.

In the absence of the Master the Senior Warden presides and has for the time being the powers and duties of the Master; in his absence the same devolve upon the Junior Warden.

All lodges have an officer stationed "without the door with a drawn sword in his hand." He is the Tiler and his duties are to keep off "cowans and eaves-droppers." In operative days the secrets of the Free-masons were valuable in coin of the realm. The Mason who knew "the Mason Word" could travel in foreign countries and receive a Master's wages. Many who could not or would not conform to the require-ments tried to ascertain the secrets in a clandestine manner.

The eavesdropper—literally, one who attempts to listen under the eaves, and so receives the droppings from the roof—was a common thief who tried to learn by stealth what he would not learn by work.

The cowan was an ignorant Mason who laid stones together without mortar or piled rough stone from the field into a wall without working them square and true. He was a Mason without the word, with no reputation; the Apprentice who tried to masquerade as a Master.

The operative Masons guarded their assemblies against the intrusion of both the thief and the half-instructed craftsman. Nothing positive is known of the date when the guardian of the door first went on duty. He was called a Tiler or Tyler because the man who put on the roof or tiles (tiler) completed the building and made those within it secure from intrusion; therefore the officer who guarded the door against intrusion was called, by analogy, a Tiler.

Lodges are referred to as Symbolic, Craft, Ancient Craft, Private, Particular, Subordinate, and Blue, all of which names distinguish them from other organizations, both Masonic and non-Masonic. The word "subordinate" is sometimes objected to by Masonic scholars, most of whom prefer other appellations to distinguish the individual Master Mason's lodge from the Grand Lodge. All Masonic lodges of Ancient Craft Masonry are "Blue Lodges"—blue being the distinctive Masonic color, from the blue vault of heaven which is the covering of a symbolic lodge, and which embraces the world, of which the lodge is a symbol.

To such an organization a man petitions for the degrees of Freemasonry. If the lodge accepts his petition a committee is appointed to investigate the petitioner. The committee reports to the lodge whether or not, in its opinion, the petitioner is suitable material out of which to make a Mason.

The statutory time of a month having elapsed and all the members of the lodge having been notified that the petition will come up for ballot at a certain stated communication (Masonic word for "meeting"), the members present ballot on the petition.

The ballot is secret and both the laws and the ancient usages and customs surrounding it are very strict. No brother is permitted to state how he will ballot or how he has balloted. No brother is permitted to inquire of another how he will or has balloted. One black cube (negative ballot) is sufficient to reject the petitioner.

The secrecy of the ballot and the universal (in this country) requirement that a ballot be unanimous to elect are two bulwarks of the Fraternity. Occasionally both the secrecy and the required unanimity may seem to work a hardship, when a man apparently worthy of being taken by the hand as a brother is rejected, but no human institution is perfect, and no human being acts always according to the best that is in him. The occasional failure of the system to work complete justice must be laid to the individuals using it and not to the Fraternity.

More will be said later in these pages on the power of the ballot, its use and abuse; here it is sufficient to note one reason for the secret and unanimous ballot by which the petitioner may be elected to receive initiation. Harmony—oneness of mind, effort, ideas, and ideals—is one of the foundations of Freemasonry. Anything which interferes with harmony hurts the institution. Therefore it is essential that lodges have a harmonious membership; that no man be admitted to the Masonic home of any brother against that brother's will.

Having passed the ballot, the petitioner in due course is notified, presents himself and is initiated.

ENTERED APPRENTICE

He then becomes an Entered Apprentice Mason. He is a Mason to the extent that he is called "brother" and has certain rights; he is not yet a Mason in the legal Masonic sense. Seeing a framework erected on a plot of ground we reply to the question, "What are they building?" by saying, "A house." We mean, "They are building something which eventually will be a house." The Entered Apprentice is a Mason only in the sense that he is a rough ashlar[1] in process of being made into a perfect ashlar.

The Entered Apprentice is the property of the lodge; he can receive his Fellowcraft and Master Mason degrees nowhere else without its permission. But he does not yet pay dues to the lodge, he is not yet permitted to sign its by-laws, he can enter it only when it is open on the first degree, he cannot hold office, vote or ballot, receive Masonic burial, attend a Masonic funeral as a member of the lodge, and has no *right* to Masonic charity.

He has the right to ask his lodge for his Fellowcraft's degree. He has the right of instruction by competent brethren to obtain that "suitable proficiency" in the work of the first degree which will entitle him to his second degree if the brethren are willing to give it to him.

The lodge asks very little of an Entered Apprentice besides the secrecy to which his obligation bound him and those exhibitions of character outlined in the Charge given at the close of the degree.

It requires that he be diligent in learning and that so far as he is able he will suit his convenience as to time and place to that of his instructors.

Inasmuch as the Rite of Destitution is taught the initiate in the first degree he may naturally wonder why an Entered Apprentice has not the right to lodge

[1] Ashlar; a building stone.

charity if he needs it. Individual Masonic charity he may, of course, receive, but the right to the organized relief of the lodge, or a Grand Lodge, belongs only to a Master Mason.

This is Masonic law; Masonic practice, in the spirit of brotherly love, would offer any relief suddenly and imperatively needed by an initiate—for that is Freemasonry.

"SUITABLE PROFICIENCY"

In the Middle Ages operative apprentices were required to laber seven years before they were thought to know enough to attempt to become Fellows of the Craft. At the end of the seven-year period an apprentice who had earned the approbation of those over him might make his Master's Piece and submit it to the judgment of the Master and Wardens of his lodge.

The Master's Piece was some difficult task of stone cutting or setting. Whether he was admitted as a Fellow or turned back for further instruction depended on its perfection.

The Master's Piece survives in Speculative Masonry only as a small task and the seven years have shrunk to a minimum of one month. Before knocking at the door of the West Gate for his Fellowcraft's Degree an Entered Apprentice must learn "by heart" a part of the ritual and the ceremonies through which he has passed.

Easy for some, difficult for others, this is an essential task. It must be done, and well done. It is no kindness to an Entered Apprentice to permit him to proceed if his Master's Piece is badly made.

ENTERED APPRENTICE

As the initiate converses with well-informed brethren, he will learn that there are literally millions of Masons in the world—three millions in the United States. He does not know them; they do not know him. Unless he can prove that he is a Mason, he cannot visit in a lodge where he is not known, neither can he apply for Masonic aid, nor receive Masonic welcome and friendship.

Hence the requirement that the Entered Apprentice learn his work well is in his own interest.

But it is also of interest to all brethren, wheresoever dispersed, that the initiate know his work. They may find it as necessary to prove themselves to him as he may need to prove himself to them. If he does not know his work, he cannot receive a proof any more than he can give it.

It is of interest to the lodge that the initiate know his work well. Well-informed Masons may be very useful in lodge; the sloppy, careless workman can never be depended upon for good work.

Appalled at the apparently great feat of memory asked, some initiates study with an instructor for an hour or two, find it difficult, and lose courage. But what millions of other men have done, any initiate can do. Any man who can learn to know by heart any two words can also learn three; having learned three he may add a fourth, and so on, until he can stand before the lodge and pass a creditable examination, or satisfy a committee that he has learned enough to entitle him to ask for further progress.

The initiate should be not only willing but enthusiastically eager to learn what is required because of its effect upon his future Masonic career. The Entered

Apprentice who wins the honor of being passed to the degree of Fellowcraft by having well performed the only task set him goes forward feeling that he is worthy. As Speculative Freemasonry builds only character, a feeling of unworthiness is as much a handicap in lodge life as a piece of faulty stone is in building a wall.

But the most important reason for learning the work thoroughly goes farther. It applies more and more as the Fellowcraft's Degree is reached and passed and is most vital after the initiate has the proud right to say, "I am a Master Mason."

RITUAL

One of the great appeals of Freemasonry, both to the profane[1] and to Masons, is its antiquity. The Order can trace an unbroken history of more than two hundred years in its present form (the Mother Grand Lodge was formed in 1717), and has irrefutable documentary evidence of a much longer existence in simpler forms.

Our present rituals—the plural is used advisedly, as no two jurisdictions are exactly at one on what is correct in ritual—are the source books from which we prove just where we came from and, to some extent, just when.

If we alter our ritual, either intentionally or by

[1] Profane: Masonically, from *pro* and *fanum*, meaning, "Without the temple." To a Mason a profane is one not a Mason; the profane world is all that is not in the Masonic world. The word as used by Masons has no relation to that used to describe what is irreligious or blasphemous.

poor memorization, we gradually lose the many references concealed in the old, old phrases which tell the story of whence we came and when.

Time is relative to the observer; what is very slow to the man may be very rapid to nature. Nature has all the time there is. To drop out a word here, put in a new one there, eliminate this sentence and add that one to our ritual seems to be a minor matter in a man's lifetime. Yet if it is continued long enough— a very few score of years—the old ritual will be entirely altered and become something new.

We have confirmation of this. Certain parts of the ritual are printed. These printed paragraphs are practically the same in most jurisdictions. Occasionally there is a variation, showing where some committee on work has not been afraid to change the work of the fathers. But as a whole the printed portion of our work is substantially what it was when it was first brought to this country more than two hundred years ago.

The secret work is very different in many of our jurisdictions. Some of these differences are accounted for by different original sources, yet even in two jurisdictions which sprang from the same source of Freemasonry, and originally had the same work, we find variations, showing that mouth-to-ear instruction, no matter how secret it may be, is not wholly an accurate way of transmitting words.

If in spite of us alterations creep in by the slow process of time and human fallibility, how much faster will the ritual change if we are careless or indifferent? The farther away we get from our original source, the more meticulously careful must trustworthy Masons be to pass on the work to posterity exactly as we receive it. The Mason of olden time could go to his source for reinspiration—we cannot.

Ritual is the thread which binds us to those who immediately preceded us, as their ritual bound them to their fathers, our grandfathers. The ritual we hand down to our sons and their sons' sons will be their bond with us, and through us with the historic dead. To alter that bond intentionally is to wrong those who come after us, even as we have been wronged when those who preceded us were careless or inefficient in their memorization of ritual.

The Entered Apprentice, then, should not be discouraged if the ritual "comes hard." He should fail not in the task nor question that it is worth while, for on what he does and on the way in which he does it depends in some measure the Freemasonry of the future. As he does well or ill, so will those who come after him do ill or well.

"FREE WILL AND ACCORD"

Though he knows it not the petitioner encounters his first Masonic symbol when he receives from the hands of a friend the petition *for which he has asked.*

Freemasons do not proselyte. The Order asks no man for his petition. Greater than any man, Freemasonry honors those she permits to knock upon her West Gate. Not king, prince, nor potentate; president, general, nor savant can honor the Fraternity by petitioning a lodge for the degrees.

Churches send out missionaries and consider it a duty to persuade men to their teachings. Commercial organizations, Boards of Trade, Chambers of Commerce, Life Insurance Associations, and so on, attempt to win members by advertising and persuasion. Members are happy to ask their friends to join their clubs. But a man must come to the West Gate of a lodge "of his own free will and accord," and can come only by the good offices of a friend whom *he* has enlisted on his behalf.

The candidate obligates himself for all time: "Once a Mason, always a Mason." He may take no interest in the Order. He may dimit,[1] become unaffiliated,[2] be dropped N. P. D.,[3] be tried for a Masonic offense and suspended or expelled, but he cannot "unmake" himself as a Mason, or ever avoid the moral responsibility of keeping the obligations he *voluntarily* assumes.

If a man be requested to join or persuaded to sign a petition, he may later be in a position to say, "I

---

[1] Dimit, also spelled demit. Masonic lexicographers quarrel as to which is correct. Dimit from the Latin *dimitto*, to permit to go, is probably more used than demit, from the Latin *demittere*, meaning to let down from an elevated position to a lower one; in other words, to resign. However spelled, in Freemasonry it signifies both the permission of the lodge to leave to join another lodge, and the paper containing that permission.

[2] Unaffiliated: a Mason who belongs to no lodge. After he has taken his dimit, a Mason is unaffiliated until again elected a member of some lodge. A brother dropped N.P.D. is unaffiliated. A man made a Mason "at sight" (done only by a Grand Master) is unaffiliated until he joins some lodge. The state of unaffiliation is Masonically frowned upon, since an unaffiliated brother contributes nothing to the Fraternity to which he is bound.

[3] N.P.D.: short for Non Payment of Dues.

became a Mason under a misapprehension. I was over-persuaded. I was argued into membership," and might thus have a self-excusing shadow of a reason for failure to do as most solemnly agrees.

But no man does so join unless he signs a false statement. He must declare in his petition, and many times during his progress through the degrees, that the act is "of my own free will and accord." Not only must he so declare, but he must so swear.

Freemasonry gives her all—and it is a great gift— to those she accepts. But she gives only to those who honestly desire the gift. He who is not first prepared to be a Freemason in his heart, that is, of his own free will and accord, can never be one.

INITIATION

"Initiation is an analogy of man's advent from prenatal darkness into the light of human fellowship, moral truth, and spiritual faith."[1]

From the Latin *initium*; a beginning, a birth, a coming into being. It is a very common human experience. We are initiated into a new world when we first go to school; adolescence is initiation into manhood or womanhood; we undergo an initiation when we plunge into business or our professions; marriage is an initiation into a new experience, a new way of living, a new outlook on life; the acceptance of a religious experience is an initiation; a new book may initiate us into a new interest. Initiation is everywhere and in one or another form comes to every man.

[1] Howard R. Cruse.

ENTERED APPRENTICE

Masonic initiation may, but does not necessarily, come to those who seek, are accepted, and receive the degrees.

Many refuse the results of initiation. The schoolboy who will not study, the man who will not work, the reader who is not interested in his book, the churchgoer to whom the service is but an empty form to be gone through once a week because "it is the thing to do"—these gain nothing from such initiations. The candidate who sees in the Masonic initiation of the Entered Apprentice Degree only a formal and dignified ceremony designed to take up an evening and push him one step forward toward membership in the Order refuses to accept his initiation.

Neither lodge nor brethren can help this. If a man will not accept what is offered, if his understanding is so dull, his mind so sodden, his imagination so dead that he cannot glimpse the substance behind the form, both he and the lodge are unlucky. That the majority of initiates do receive and take to themselves this opportunity for spiritual rebirth is obvious, otherwise the Order would not live and grow, could not have lived through hundreds—in some form, thousands—of years.

He is a wise initiate who will read and study that he may receive *all* of that for which he has asked. The lodge puts before him the bread of truth, the wine of belief, the staff of power, and sets his feet upon the path that leads to Light . . . but it is for him to eat and drink and travel the winding path of initiation which at long last leads to the symbolic East.

INTRODUCTION TO FREEMASONRY

THE LODGE AS A SYMBOL

The lodge is a symbol of the world. Its shape, the "oblong square," is the ancient conception of the shape of the world. The Entered Apprentice is taught its dimensions, its covering, its furniture, its lights, its jewels, and will learn more of it as a symbol as he proceeds through the degrees. Although a symbol of the world, the lodge is a world unto itself; a world within a world, different in its customs, its laws, and its structure from the world without. In the world without are class distinctions, wealth, power, poverty, and misery. In the lodge all are on a level and peace and harmony prevail. In the world without most laws are "thou shalt not" and enforced by penalties. In the lodge the laws are mostly "thou shalt" and compulsion is seldom thought of and as rarely invoked. Freemasons obey their laws not so much because they must as because they will. In the world without men are divided by a thousand influences: race, business, religious belief, politics. In the lodge men are united in the common bond of three fundamental beliefs: the Fatherhood of God, the brotherhood of man and the immortality of the soul, and all the sweet associations which spring therefrom. In the world without men travel many roads to many goals; in the lodge the initiate does as all others who have gone this way before him, and all, youngest Entered Apprentice and oldest Past Master, travel a common way to an end which is the same for all.

PREPARATION

Often it seems queer to the candidate. How should

it not, when he receives his explanations afterwards and not before? When the Entered Apprentice Degree is concluded, the initiate who has ears to hear knows some of the reasons for the manner of his preparation and reception, although he should read not only this but larger books which will amplify these instructions to his betterment. He may well begin with the Book of Ruth, in which he will find much illumination "concerning their manner of redeeming and changing."

But the Rite of Discalceation,[1] as it is called, has another significance than that of giving testimony of sincerity of intentions. These are sufficiently important; a candidate for the Entered Apprentice Degree who is not sincere will have a very disagreeable time in Freemasonry. But the hidden meaning of the rite is perhaps even more important than the explained meaning. Here the initiate must possess his soul in patience. He is not yet wholly admitted to the temple which is Freemasonry. He is not permitted to do as Master Masons do, or to know what Master Masons know. For the whole Masonic significance of the rite he must wait until it is his privilege to receive the Sublime Degree of Master Mason.

It should not come as a surprise that a special preparation for initiation is required. The soldier's uniform allows his greatest freedom of action. The bridegroom dresses in his best. The knight of old put on shining armor when going into battle. Men prepare in some way, to the best of their ability, for any new experience.

[1] From the Latin *discalceatus;* unshod.

Preparation for Masonic initiation is wholly a symbolic matter, but with deeper meanings and greater than are apparent on first acquaintance.

CIRCUMAMBULATION

This mouthful of a word, meaning literally "walking around," is not only the name of a part of a degree but also of a symbol. The candidate is conducted around the lodge room for a reason later explained, but the inner meaning of this ceremony is hidden. Its deep significance unites the initiate not only with all who have gone this way before in a Masonic lodge, but with those uncounted millions of men who for thousands of years have made of circumambulation an offering of homage to the Unseen Presence.

Among the first religions were sun and fire worship. Prehistoric man found God in nature. Thunder was His voice; lightning was His weapon; wind was His breath; fire was His presence. The sun gave light and heat; it kept away the wild beasts; it grew the crops; it was life itself. Fire gave light and heat and prepared the food—it, also, was life itself. Worship of the sun in the sky was conducted symbolically by worship of fire upon piles of stones which were the first altars.

Man is incurably imitative. The small boy struts with his father's cane; the little girl puts on her mother's dress to play grown up; the valet imitates the master; the clerk imitates his manager. Early man imitated the God he worshiped. Heat and light he could give by fire, so lighting the fire on the altar became an important religious ceremony. And early man could imitate the movements of his God.

The sun seems to move from east to west by way of the south. Early man circled altars, on which burned the fire which was his God, from east to west by way of the south. Circumambulation became a part of all religious observances; it was in the ceremonies of ancient Egypt; it was part of the mysteries of Eleusis; it was practiced in the rites of Mithras and a thousand other cults, and down through the ages it has come to us.

When the candidate first circles the lodge room about the altar, he walks step by step with a thousand shades of men who have thus worshiped the Most High by humble imitation. Thus thought of circumambulation is no longer a mere parade but a ceremony of significance, linking all who take part in it with the spiritual aspirations of a dim and distant past.

A further significant teaching of this symbol is its introduction to the idea of dependence. Freemasonry speaks plainly here to him who listens. Of this Newton[1] has beautifully written:

> From the hour we are born till we are laid in the grave we grope our way in the dark, and none could find or keep the path without a guide. From how many ills, how many perils, how many pitfalls we are guarded in the midst of the years!

[1] Dr. Joseph Fort Newton: an Episcopal minister whose golden pen has given to Freemasonry *The Builders*, *The Men's House*, *The Religion of Masonry*, *Short Talks on Masonry*, and whose vision and inspiration are a power in the Masonic world.

INTRODUCTION TO FREEMASONRY

With all our boasted wisdom and foresight, even when we fancy we are secure, we may be in the presence of dire danger, if not of death itself.

Truly it does not lie in man to direct his path, and without a true and trusted friend in whom we can confide, not one of us would find his way home. So Masonry teaches us, simply but unmistakably, at the first step as at the last, that we live and walk by faith, not by sight; and to know that fact is the beginning of wisdom. Since this is so, since no man can find his way alone, in life as in the lodge we must in humility trust our Guide, learn His ways, follow Him and fear no danger. Happy is the man who has learned that secret.

UNITY

In an Entered Apprentice's Lodge, the 133rd Psalm is read—sometimes sung—during the course of the degree:

Behold, how good and how pleasant it is for brethren to dwell together in unity. .It is like the precious ointment upon the head, that ran down upon the beard, even Aaron's beard; that went down to the skirts of his garments; As the dew of Hermon and as the dew that descended upon the mountains of Zion, for there the Lord commanded the blessing, even life for evermore.

Unity is an essential of a Masonic lodge. Unity of thought, of intention, of execution. It is l ut another word for harmony, which Freemasons are taught is the strength and support of all well-regulated institutions, especially this of ours. Dew is nature's blessing where little rain falls; the dew of Hermon is proverbially heavy. Israel poured precious ointments on the heads of those the people honored; that which went down to the skirts of his garments was evidently great in quantity, significant of the honor paid to Aaron, personification of high priesthood, representative of the solidity of his group. The whole passage is a glorification of the beauty of brotherly love, which is why it was anciently selected to be a part of the Entered Apprentice's Degree, in which the initiate is first introduced to that principal tenet of the Fraternity.

SECRECY

In the true sense of the words Freemasonry is not a secret society but a society with secrets. A secret society is one the members of which are not known; a society which exists without common knowledge. Freemasonry is well known. Men proudly wear the emblem of the Order on coat and watch charm and ring. Many Grand Lodges publish lists of their members. Many Grand Lodges maintain card indexes of all members in the jurisdiction so that it is easy to ascertain whether or not a man is a Mason. Grand Lodges publish their Proceedings, a Masonic press caters to the Masonic world, and thousands of books have been written about Freemasonry. Obviously it is not the society which is secret.

The initiate takes an obligation of secrecy; if he will carefully consider the language of that obligation, he will see that it concerns the forms and ceremonies, the manner of teaching, certain modes of recognition. There is no obligation of secrecy regarding the *truths* taught by Freemasonry, otherwise such a book as this could not lawfully be written.

Sometimes the question is asked by a profane, "Why have *any* secrets? If what you know and teach is worth so much, why not give it to the world?"

Secrecy is a common fact of everyday life. Our private affairs are *ours*, not to be shouted from the housetops. Business secrets are often of value in proportion to the success of keeping them. Diplomacy is necessarily conducted in secret. Board meetings of companies, banks, business houses, are secret. A man and his wife have private understandings for no one else to know. The lover tells the secrets of his heart to but one ear.

From all of us some things are secret and hidden that might be open and known—if we had the wit or would take the trouble to learn. Fine music is a secret from the tone deaf. Mathematics are a secret from the ignorant. Philosophy is a secret from the commonplace mind. Freemasonry is a secret from the profane—and for the same reasons!

The secrecy of Masonry is an honorable secrecy; any good man may ask for her secrets; those who are worthy will receive them. To give them to those who do not seek, or who are not worthy, would but impoverish the Fraternity and enrich not those who received them.

It is sometimes suggested that Freemasonry pretends to possess valuable secrets merely to intrigue men to apply for them through curiosity. How mistaken this is is understood by every Freemason. He who seeks Freemasonry out of curiosity for her secrets must be bitterly disappointed. In school the teacher is anxious to instruct all who seek the classroom in the secrets of geometry, but not all students wish to study geometry and not all who do have the wit to comprehend. Freemasonry is anxious to give of her secrets to worthy men fit to receive them but not all are worthy, and not all the worthy seek.

PENALTIES

Freemasonry has been aptly described as "the gentle Craft." Its teachings are of brotherly love, relief, truth, love of God, charity, immortality, mutual help, sympathy. To the initiate, therefore, the penalty in his obligation comes often with a shock of surprise and sometimes consternation.

Let it be said with emphasis: *the penalties are wholly symbolic.*

The small boy uses the expression "By golly," keeping alive an ancient Cornish oath in which *goll* or the hand, uplifted, was offered as a sacrifice if what was said was not the truth. In our courts of law we say, "So help me, God," in taking the oath to tell the truth. But the small boy does not expect his hand to be cut off if he happens to fib, nor is the penalty for perjury such that only God may help him upon whom it is inflicted.

Masonic penalties go back to very ancient times; to years when punishments were cruel and inhuman, often for very small offenses. Throats were cut, tongues torn out, bodies cut in half, hooks struck into breasts and the body torn apart; men were dismembered for all sorts of offenses which seem to us much too trivial for such extreme punishments; looting a temple, stealing a sheep, disclosing the king's secrets, etc.

Other punishments of the Middle Ages were based on religious fears. To be buried in unconsecrated ground was a terrible end for ignorant and superstitious people who believed that it meant eternal damnation. Similarly, to be interred in land which was no man's property—between high and low water mark—was symbolical of spiritual death.

These and other horrible penalties were inflicted by law by various peoples at various times. That the legal penalties for certain civil crimes were incorporated in Masonic obligations seems obvious. But that they ever meant or were ever intended to mean any death but a symbolic one is simply not so.

The yokel who cries "May God strike me dead if this is not so" does not mean that he wishes to die; but he says that he believes he will be worthy of death if he lies. It is in such a way that the Masonic penalties are to be understood; the Entered Apprentice states his belief that he would merit the penalty of his obligation if he failed to keep it.

The only punishments ever inflicted by Freemasons upon Freemasons are reprimand, suspension (definite and indefinite), and expulsion from the Fraternity. The initiate who violates his obligation will feel the weight of no hand laid upon him. He will suffer no physical penalties whatever. The contempt and detestation of his brethren, their denial of the privileges of Freemasonry to the foresworn, are the only Masonic penalties ever inflicted.

ENTERED APPRENTICE

There are three—the Holy Bible, the Square, and the Compasses.[1]

The Holy Bible is always referred to as "The Great Light" or "The Great Light in Masonry," in this country which is predominantly Christian. The practice may be and often is different in other lands. What is vital and unchangeable, a Landmark of the Order (a further discussion of Landmarks is given later, *see* pages 159–163) is that a *Volume of the Sacred Law be open upon the Masonic altar whenever the lodge is open.* A lodge wholly Jewish may prefer to use only the Old Testament; in Turkey and Persia the Koran would be used as the V. S. L. of the Mohammedan; Brahmins would use the Vedas. In the Far East where Masonic lodges have members of many races and creeds it is customary to have several holy books upon the altar that the initiate may choose that which is to him the most sacred.

The Holy Bible, our Great Light in Masonry, is opened upon our altars. Upon it lie the other Great Lights—the Square and the Compasses. Without all three no Masonic lodge can exist, much less open or work. Together with the warrant from the Grand Lodge they are indispensable.

The Bible on the altar is more than the rule and guide of our faith. It is one of the greatest of Freemasonry's symbols. For the Bible is here a symbol of all holy books of all faiths. It is the Masonic way of setting forth that simplest and most profound of truths which Masonry has made so peculiarly her

[1] "Compass" in six jurisdictions.

own: that there *is* a way, there *does* run a road on which men "of all creeds and of every race" may travel happily together, be their differences of religious faith what they may. In his private devotions a man may petition God or Jehovah, Allah or Buddha, Mohammed or Jesus; he may call upon the God of Israel or the Great First Cause. In the Masonic Lodge he hears humble petition to the Great Architect of the Universe, finding his own deity under that name.

A hundred paths may wind upward around a mountain; at the top they meet. Freemasonry opens the Great Light upon her altar not as one book of one faith, but as all books of all faiths, the book of the Will of the Great Architect, read in what language, what form, what shape we will. It is as all-inclusive as the symbols which lie upon it. The Square is not for any one lodge, any one nation, any one religion— it is for all Masons, everywhere, to all of whom it speaks the same tongue. The Compasses circumscribe the desires of Masons wheresoever dispersed; the secret of the Square, held between the points of the Compasses (*see* page 58) is universal.

Countless references in our ritual are taken from the Old Testament. Almost every name in a Masonic lodge is from the Scriptures. In the Great Light are found those simple teachings of the universality of brotherhood, the love of God for his children, the hope of immortality, which are the very warp and woof of Freemasonry. Let it be emphasized; these are the teachings of Freemasonry in every tongue, in every land, for those of every faith. Our Great Light is but a symbol of the Volume of the Sacred Law. Freemasonry is no more a Christian organization than it is Jewish or Mohammedan or Brahmin. Its use of the collection of sacred writings of the Jews (Old Testament) and the Gospels of the New Testament as the Great Light must not confuse the initiate so that he reads into Freemasonry a sectarian character which is not there.

This is so well understood that it needs emphasis only for the novice. To give him specific facts as well as assertion: the Bible is first mentioned as a Great Light in Masonry about 1760, whereas the first of the Old Charges (one of the foundation stones on which rest the laws of Freemasonry, first published in 1723, but presumably adopted by the Mother Grand Lodge at its formation in 1717) reads in part as follows (spelling modernized):

> A Mason is obliged by his tenure to obey the moral law; and if he rightly understands the art, he will never be a stupid atheist, nor an irreligious libertine. But though in ancient times Masons were charged in every country to be of the religion of that country or nation, whatever it was, yet 'tis now thought more expedient only to oblige them to that religion in which all men agree, leaving their particular opinions to themselves; that is, to be good men and true, or men of honor and honesty, by whatever denominations or persuasions they may be distinguished; whereby Masonry becomes the center of union and the means of conciliating true friendship among persons that must have remained at a perpetual distance.

Perhaps never before has so short a paragraph had

so profound an effect, setting forth the non-sectarian, non-doctrinal character of Freemasonry, making religion, not *a* religion, the important matter in the Ancient Craft.

CABLE TOW

In old rituals this was originally "cable rope." Our cable tow probably comes from the German "Kabel tau."

The cable tow is symbolic of that life cord by which the infant receives life from his mother. Symbolically the cable tow is the cord by which the Masonic infant is attached to his Mother Lodge. When a baby is born the physical cord is severed but never the knife was ground which can cut the spiritual cord which ties a man to his mother. In the Entered Apprentice Degree the physical restraint of the cable tow is removed as soon as the spiritual bond of the obligation is assumed but never the means has been made by which to cut the obligation which binds a man to his Mother Lodge and the gentle Craft. Expulsion does not release from the obligation; unaffiliation does not dissolve the tie; dimitting and joining another lodge cannot make of the new lodge the Mother Lodge.

The cable tow has further significance in the succeeding degrees which will be discussed later.

THE LESSER LIGHTS

When an initiate is first brought to light, the radiance comes from the three Lesser Lights, which form a triangle about or near the altar. Lesser Lights are lit when the lodge is opened and the altar arranged and extinguished when the lodge is closed and the Great Lights displaced. Something—not very much— is said of them in the ritual. They form one of those symbols in Freemasonry . . . of which there are so many! . . . which the individual brother is supposed to examine and translate for himself, getting from it what he can and enjoying what he gets in direct proportion to the amount of labor and thought he is willing to devote to the process of extracting the meaning from the outer covering.

In some jurisdictions the Lesser Lights are closely about the altar: in others one is placed at each of the stations of the three principal officers. In some lodges the three Lesser Lights form a right, in others an equilateral, in others an isosceles triangle. What is uniform throughout the Masonic world is the triangular formation; what is different is the shape and size of the triangle.

Of course, it is not possible to place three lights to form anything else but a triangle; they cannot be made to form a square or a star. Hence the natural question: why are there *three* Lesser Lights and not two or four or more?

There is "three" throughout Ancient Craft Masonry. The first of the great Sacred Numbers of the Ancient Mysteries, three was the numerical symbol of God, but *not* because God was necessarily considered as triune. While many religions of many ages and peoples have conceived of Divinity as a trinity, the figure three as a symbol of God is far older than any trinitarian doctrine. The triangle, like the circle, is without beginning or ending. One line, or two lines, have ends. They start and finish. Like the square or the five or more sided figure, the triangle has *no* loose ends. And the triangle is the *first* of these which can be made; as God was always considered as first, and also as without either beginning or ending, the triangle itself soon became a symbol of Deity.

Ancient peoples made much of sex. Their two greatest impulses were self-preservation and mating. Their third was protection of children. So powerful were these in primal man that not all his civilization, his luxury, his complicated and involved life, have succeeded in removing them as the principal mainsprings of all human endeavor. It was natural for the savage worshiper of a shining god in the sky to think he, too, required a mate, especially when that mate was so plainly in evidence. The Moon became the Sun's bride by a process of reasoning as plain as it was childlike.

Father, mother . . . there must be a child, of course. That child was Mercury, the nearest planet to the sun, the one the god kept closest to him. Here we have the origin of the three Lesser Lights; in earliest recorded accounts of the Mysteries of Eleusis (to mention only one) we find three lights about the holy place, representing the Sun, the Moon, and Mercury.

The Worshipful Master rules and governs his lodge as truly as the Sun and Moon rule and govern day and night. There can be no lodge without a Worshipful Master; he is, in a very real sense, the lodge itself. There are some things he cannot do that the brethren under him can do. But without him the brethren can do nothing, while without the brethren's consent or even their assistance, he can do much. As one of the principal functions of the Worshipful Master is to give "good and wholesome instruction" to his lodge, the inclusion of one light as his symbol is but a logical carrying out of that Masonic doctrine which makes the East the source of Masonic light to the brethren.

By the light of the Lesser Lights the Entered Apprentice is led to see those objects which mean so much to a Mason, the Great Lights; the inestimable gift of God to man as the rule and guide for his faith and practice, the tools dedicated to the Craft and to the Master, the Alpha and Omega of Freemasonry. Light alone is not enough; light must be *used!* Here, too, is symbolism which it is well to muse upon.

As the lodge as a whole is a symbol of the world, so should a Mason's heart be to him always a symbol of the lodge. In it he should carry ever what he may remember of the Great Light and with spiritual compasses lay out his work; with spiritual square, square both work and actions toward all mankind, "more especially a brother Mason." Therefore must he carry also in his heart three tiny Lesser Lights, by the light of which he uses his spiritual lodge furnishings. If he lights these from the torch of love and burns one for friendliness, one for helpfulness and one for godliness, he will be truly an initiate in the real sense of that term, and about the altar of Freemasonry find a new satisfaction in the new meanings which the three Lesser Lights will, with silent light and soft, imprint upon his heart.

INTRODUCTION TO FREEMASONRY

Mackey[1] states, "A mode of recognition which derives its name from its object, which is to duly guard the person using it."

Other commentators have seen it as derived from the French "Dieu Garde"—God guard me.

The origin of the Third Perfect Point is taught in the degree. Its use, in salute, is a silent way of saying to all present, "I remember my obligation; I am conscious of the penalty of its violation; I forget not my duty."

The initiate uses it first in a salutation to the Wardens, a ceremony the significance of which should never be forgotten. The government of a Masonic lodge is tripartite; it is in the hands of a Master and two Wardens. By this ceremony the Entered Apprentice admits their authority, submits himself to their government under the Master, and agrees to abide by their setting mauls when it is proper for them to use them.

The Due Guard is given by an Entered Apprentice on entering and retiring, that he may never forget the significance of his position when he took upon

[1] Albert Gallatin Mackey: one of the greatest students and most widely followed authorities the Masonic world has known. His *Encyclopedia of Freemasonry* is a standard work; his *Jurisprudence* and his *Symbolism*, if materially added to and changed since his time, are yet foundation works. His *History* is exhaustive; his List of Landmarks, if often superseded in these more modern days, first reduced the vexed question to proportions in which it might be grasped by the average Masonic mind. The Entered Apprentice who pursues his studies in Freemasonry may do much worse than consult the great Master of Freemasonry.

himself that obligation which gave him the title, Brother.

THE LAMBSKIN APRON

More ancient than the Golden Fleece or Roman Eagle, more honorable than the Star and Garter . . .

In these words the ritual seeks to impress upon him who has been invested with the white lambskin apron its value and its importance.

The Order of the Golden Fleece was founded by Philip, Duke of Burgundy, in 1429.

The Roman Eagle was Rome's symbol and ensign of power and might a hundred years before Christ.

The Order of the Star was created by John II of France in the middle of the Fourteenth Century.

The Order of the Garter was founded by Edward III of England in 1349 for himself and twenty-five Knights of the Garter.

It is commonly supposed that the apron became the "badge of a Mason" because stonemasons wore aprons to protect their clothing from the rough contact of building material. But the apron is far, far older than Golden Fleece or Roman Eagle, than the Star or Garter, than the stonemasons of the Middle Ages—aye, older than the Comacine Masters, the *Collegia* of Rome, the Dionysian Artificers who preceded them.

The Hebrew prophets wore aprons and the high priests were so decorated. In the mysteries of Egypt and of India aprons were worn as symbols of priestly power. The earliest Chinese secret societies used aprons; the Essenes wore them, as did the Incas of Peru and the Aztecs of Mexico.

INTRODUCTION TO FREEMASONRY

Throughout the Old Testament are references to lambs, often in connection with sacrifices, frequently used in a sense symbolic of innocence, purity, gentleness, weakness, a matter aided by color, which we unconsciously associate with purity, probably because of the hue of snow.

This association is universal in Freemasonry, and the initiate should strive to keep his apron white and himself innocent. His badge of a Mason should symbolize in its color the purity of his Masonic character; he should forever be innocent of wrong toward all but "more especially a brother Mason."

With the presentation of the apron the lodge accepts the initiate as worthy. It entrusts to his hands its distinguishing badge. With it and symbolized by it comes one of the most precious and most gracious of gifts: the gift of brotherhood. Lucky the Entered Apprentice who has the wit to see the extent and the meaning of the gift; thrice lucky the lodge whose initiates find in it and keep that honor, probity and power, that innocence, strength, and spiritual contact, that glory of unity and oneness with all the Masonic world which may be read into this symbol by him who hath open eyes of the heart with which to see. In the words of the Old Dundee Lodge[1] Apron Charge:

It is yours to wear throughout an honorable life, and at your death to be placed upon the coffin which shall contain your mortal remains and with them laid beneath the silent clods of the valley. Let its pure and spotless surface be to you an ever-present reminder of a purity of life and rectitude of conduct, a never-ending

[1] Of Scotland.

40

argument for nobler deeds, for higher thoughts, for greater achievements. And when at last your weary feet shall have come to the end of their toilsome journey, and from your nerveless grasp shall drop the working tools of life, may the record of your thoughts and actions be as pure and spotless as this emblem . . .

For thus, and thus only, may it be worn with pleasure to yourself and honor to the Fraternity.

"THE GREATEST OF THESE"

The Entered Apprentice practices the Rite of Destitution before he hears the beautiful words of the lecture descriptive of the three principal rounds of Jacob's ladder: "the greatest of these is charity; for faith is lost in sight, hope ends in fruition, but charity extends beyond the grave, through the boundless realms of eternity." But he may reflect upon both at once and from that reflection learn that Masonic giving to the destitute is not confined to alms.

Putting a quarter in a beggar's hand will hardly extend beyond the grave through the boundless realms of eternity!

Masonic charity does indeed include the giving of physical relief; individual Masons give it, the lodge gives it, the Grand Lodge gives it. But if charity began and ended with money, it would go but a little way. St. Paul said: "And although I bestow all my goods to feed the poor and have not charity, it profiteth me nothing."

If the charity of Freemasonry meant only the giving of alms, it would long ago have given place to a hundred institutions better able to provide relief.

The charity taught in the lodge is charity of thought, charity of the giving of self. The visit to the sick is true Masonic charity. The brotherly hand laid upon a bowed shoulder in comfort and to give courage is Masonic charity. The word of counsel to the fatherless, the tear dropped in sympathy with the widowed, the joyous letter of congratulation to a fortunate brother, all are Masonic charity—and these, indeed, extend beyond the grave.

Often an Entered Apprentice believes that the Rite has taught him that every Mason must give a coin to every beggar who asks, even though they line the streets and need as many dimes as a pocket will hold. Such is not the truth. The Mason gives when he meets anyone "in like destitute condition." It is left for him to judge whether the appeal is for a need which is real or one assumed. In general all calls for Masonic charity should be made through the lodge; machinery is provided for a kindly and brotherly investigation, after which lodge or Grand Lodge will afford relief. Individual charity is wholly in the control of the individual brother's conscience.

But no conscience need control that larger and finer giving of comfort and counsel, of joy and sadness, of sympathy and spiritual help. Here the Mason may give as much as he will and be not the poorer but the richer for his giving. He who reads the Rite of Destitution in this larger sense has seen through the form to the reality behind and learned the inner significance of the symbol.

NORTHEAST

Cornerstones are laid in the Northeast Corner because the Northeast is the point of beginning; midway between the darkness of the North and the light of the East.

The Entered Apprentice lays his Masonic Cornerstone standing in the Northeast corner of the lodge, midway between the darkness of profane ignorance and the full light of the symbolic East.

Here, if indeed he be a man of imagination and no clod, he receives a thrill that may come to him never again—save once only—in Masonry. For here he enters into his heritage as an Entered Apprentice. All that has gone before has been queer, mysterious, puzzling, almost mind-shocking, devastating with its newness and its differences from the world he knows. Now he stands "a just and upright Mason" to receive those first instructions which, well studied, will enable him to understand what has been done with and to him as to all who have gone this way before.

Never again will he stand here, an Entered Apprentice—a man receives the degree but once. Never, therefore, should he forget that once he stood there, nor how he stood there, nor why. And if, momentarily, memory leaves him, let him look in the Great Light and read (Ezekiel ii, 1–2):

And God said unto me, Son of Man, stand upon thy feet and I will speak unto thee. And the spirit entered into me when he spake unto me, and set me upon my feet, that I heard him that spake unto me.

No man stands in the Northeast Corner with his heart open but hears that Voice which thundered to the prophet of old.

WORKING TOOLS

The Entered Apprentice receives from the hands of the Master two working tools.

The Twenty-four Inch Gauge is well explained in the ritual, but the significance of one point is sometimes overlooked. The Entered Apprentice is taught that by the Twenty-four Inch Gauge he should divide his time: "Eight hours for the service of God and a distressed worthy brother; eight for the usual vocations, and eight for refreshment and sleep."

There is no time to be wasted. There is no time to be idle. There is no time for waiting.

The implication is plain; the Entered Apprentice should be always ready to use his tools. He should recall the words of Flavius to the workman in *Julius Caesar*, "Where is thy leather apron and thy rule? What does thou with thy best apparel on?" Freemasonry is not only for the lodge room but for life. Not to take the Twenty-four Inch Gauge into the profane world and by its divisions number the hours for the working of a constructive purpose is to miss the practical application of Masonic labor and Masonic charity.

The Common Gavel which "breaks off the corners of rough stones, the better to fit them for the builder's use" joins the Rough and Perfect Ashlars in a hidden symbol of the Order at once beautiful and tender. The famous sculptor and ardent Freemason, Gutzon Borglum, asked how he carved stone into beautiful statues, once said, "It is very simple. I merely knock away with hammer and chisel the stone I do not need and the statue is there—*it was there all the time.*"

In the Great Light we read: "The kingdom of heaven is within you." We are also there taught that man is made in the image of God. As Brother Borglum has so beautifully said, images are made by a process of taking away. The perfection is already within. All that is required is to remove the roughness, the excrescences, "divesting our hearts and consciences of all the vices and superfluities of life" to show forth the perfect man and Mason within. Thus the gavel becomes also the symbol of personal power.

The Common Gavel has in every lodge a still further significance; it is the symbol of the authority of the Worshipful Master. Later the initiate will learn of the great extent of the power vested in the Master of a lodge; sufficient now to say that the wise Master uses his power sparingly and never arbitrarily. While the peace and harmony of the Craft are maintained, he need not use it except as the ritual or custom of presiding in the lodge requires. If he so use it it will be respected and its possessor will be venerated.

The Master always retains possession of the gavel and never allows it beyond reach. He carries it with him when he moves about the lodge in process of conferring a degree. When the lodge is in charge of the Junior Warden at refreshment[1] it is the Junior Warden who uses a gavel to control the lodge. The gavel is the Master's symbol of authority and reminds him that although his position is the highest within the gift of the brethren, he is yet but a brother among brethren. Holding the highest power in the lodge he

[1] Masonic word for "at ease," meaning "not at work, but not closed."

45

exercises it by virtue of the commonest of the working tools.

Like all great symbols the gavel takes upon itself in the minds of the brethren something of the quality of the thing symbolized. As we revere the cotton in stripes and stars which become the flag of our country; as we revere the paper and ink which become the Great Light in Masonry, so, also, do Freemasons revere the Common Gavel which typifies and symbolizes the height of Masonic authority—the majesty of power, the wisdom of Light which rest in and shine forth from the Oriental Chair.

IMMOVABLE JEWELS

No symbol in all Freemasonry has the universal significance of the Square. It is the typical jewel; the emblem known the world over as the premier implement of the stone worker and the most important of the Masonic working tools.

Every schoolboy learns that an angle of ninety degrees is a right angle. So common is the description that few—even few Masons—pause in busy lives to ask why. The ninety-degree angle is not only *a* right angle, but it is *the* right angle—the only angle which is "right" for stones which will form a wall, a building, a cathedral. Any other angle is, Masonically, incorrect.

About the symbolism of the Square is nothing abstruse. Stonemasons use it to prove the Perfect Ashlars. If the stone fits the square, it is ready for the builder's use. Hence the words "try square" and hence, too, the universal significance of the word "square," meaning moral, upright, honorable, fair dealing.

Five centuries before the Christian era—to mention only one ancient use of the Square as an emblem of morality—a Chinese author wrote a book called *The Great Learning*. In it is the negative of the Golden Rule, that a man should not do unto others that which he does not wish others to do unto him. And then the Chinese sage adds, "This is called the principle of acting on the Square."

The initiate walks around the lodge turning corners on the square. On the altar is again the Square. He sees the Square hung about the neck of the Master —particularly is the Square the jewel of the Master, because from him must come all Masonic light to his brethren, and his teachings must be "square." The Square shares with the Level and the Plumb the quality of immovability in the lodge, meaning that as it is always the jewel of the Master, so is it immovably in the Symbolic East. An emblem of virtue, it is always in sight of the brethren in the lodge; for him who carries his Masonry into his daily life, it is forever in sight within, the try square of conscience, the tool by which he squares his every act and word.

The Level and the Plumb are the other Immovable Jewels; the Level worn by the Senior Warden in the West, the Plumb by the Junior Warden in the South. While Square, Level and Plumb are Immovable Jewels and as such belong to all three of the degrees of Ancient Craft Masonry; while all are always worn by the three principal officers and all are first seen and noted in the Entered Apprentice's Degree, they have a further significance in the second or Fellowcraft's Degree, and the Plumb has an especial signifi-cance in that ceremony.

NORTH, PLACE OF DARKNESS

The reference to the ecliptic has puzzled many a brother who has not studied the elements of astronomy.

The earliest astronomers defined the ecliptic as the hypothetical "circular" plane of the earth's path about the sun with the sun in the "center."

As a matter of fact the sun is not in the center and the earth's path about the sun is not circular. The earth travels once about the sun in three hundred and sixty-five days and a fraction, on an *elliptic* path; the sun is at one of the foci of that ellipse.

The axis of the earth, about which it turns once in twenty-four hours, thus making a night and day, is inclined to this hypothetical plane by 23½ degrees. At one point in its yearly path the north pole of the earth is inclined toward the sun by this amount. Halfway farther around its path the north pole is in-clined away from the sun by this angle. The longest day in the northern hemisphere—June 21—occurs when the north pole is most inclined toward the sun.

Any building situated between latitudes 23½ north and 23½ south of the equator will receive the rays of the sun at meridian (noon) from the north at some time during the year. King Solomon's Temple at Jerusalem, being in latitude 31 degrees 47 seconds north, lay beyond this limit. At no time in the year, therefore, did the sun or moon at meridian "dart its rays into the northerly portion thereof."

ENTERED APPRENTICE

As astronomy in Europe is comparatively modern some have argued that this reason for considering the North, Masonically, as a place of darkness, must be also comparatively modern. This is wholly mistaken—Pythagoras (to go no further back) recognized the obliquity of the world's axis to the ecliptic, as well as that the earth was a sphere suspended in space. While Pythagoras (born 586 B.C.) is younger than Solomon's Temple, he is almost two thousand years older than the beginnings of astronomy in Europe.

POINT WITHIN A CIRCLE

There is in every regular and well-governed Lodge, a certain point within a circle, embordered by two perpendicular parallel lines. . . .

It is among the most illuminating of the Entered Apprentice's symbols and is important not only for its antiquity, and many meanings which have been read from it, but because of the bond it makes between the old operative stone setter's art and the Speculative Masonry we know.

No man may say when, where, or how the symbol began. From the earliest dawn of history a simple closed figure has been man's symbol for Deity—the circle for some peoples, the triangle for others, and a circle or a triangle with a central point for still others. In some jurisdictions a lodge closes with brethren forming a circle about the altar, which thus becomes the point or focus of the Supreme Blessing upon the brethren.

A symbol may have many meanings, all of them

right, so long as they are not self-contradictory. As the point within a circle has had so many different meanings to so many different people, it is natural that it have many meanings for Masons.

It is connected with sun worship, the most ancient of religions; ruins of ancient temples devoted both to sun and to fire worship are circular in form with a central altar or point which was the Holy of Holies. The symbol is found in India in which land of mystery and mysticism its antiquity is beyond calculation. In ancient meaning the point represents the sun and the circle the universe. This is both modern and ancient, as a dot in a small circle is the astronomical symbol for the sun.

The two parallel lines which in modern Masonry represent the two holy Sts. John are as ancient as the rest of the symbol, but originally had nothing to do with the "two eminent Christian patrons of Masonry." They date back to an era before Solomon. On early Egyptian monuments may be found the Alpha and Omega or symbol of God in the center of a circle embordered by two perpendicular, parallel *serpents* representing the Power and the Wisdom of the Creator.

This is not only a symbol of creation but is fraught with other meanings. When man conceived that fire, water, the sun, the moon, the stars, the lightning, the thunder, the mountains and rivers did not each have a special deity, that in all this universe there was but *one* God, and wanted to draw a picture of that conception of unity, the only thing he could do was to make a point. When man conceived that God was eternal, without beginning and without ending, from everlasting to everlasting, and desired to draw a picture of that conception of eternity, he could but draw a circle that goes around and around forever. When man conceived that the Master Builder did not blow hot and cold, that he was not changing, fickle and capricious, but a God of rectitude and justice, and needed to picture that conception of righteousness, he drew straight up and down parallel lines. So this symbol stands for the unity, the eternal life, and the righteousness of God.

That derivation of the symbol which best satisfies the mind as to logic and appropriateness students find in the operative craft. The tools used by the cathedral builders were the same as ours to-day; they had gavel and mallet, setting maul and hammer, chisel and trowel, plumb and square, level and twenty-four inch gauge to "measure and lay out their work."

The square, the level, and the plumb were made of wood—wood, cord, and weight for plumb and level; wood alone for square.

Wood wears when used against stone and warps when exposed to water or damp air. The metal used to fasten the two arms of the square together would rust and perhaps bend or break. Naturally the squares would not stay square indefinitely but had to be checked up constantly for their right-angledness.

The importance of the perfect right angle in the square by which the stones were shaped can hardly be overestimated. Operative Masonry in the cathedral-building days was largely a matter of cut and try, of individual workmen, of careful craftsmanship. Quantity production, micrometer measurement, interchangeable parts had not been invented. All the more necessary then that the foundation on which all the work was done should be as perfect as the Masters knew how to make it. Cathedral builders erected their temples for all time—how well they built a hundred glorious structures in the Old World testify. They built well because they knew how to check and try their squares.

Draw a circle—any size—on a piece of paper. With a straight edge draw a line through its center. Put a dot on the circle anywhere. Connect that dot with the line at both points where it crosses the circle. Result, a perfect right angle. Draw the circle of what size you will; place the dot on the circumference where you will; if the lines from the dot meet the horizontal line crossing the circle through its center, they will form a right angle.

This was the operative Master's great secret—knowing how to "try the square." It was by this means that he tested working tools; did he do so often enough it was impossible either for tools or work "to materially err." From this also comes the ritual used in the lodges of our English brethren where they "open on the center."

The original line across the center has been shifted to the side and become the "two perpendicular parallel lines" of Egypt and India, and our admonitions are no longer what they must once have been; . . . "while a Mason circumscribes his *square* within these points, it is impossible that *it* should materially err." But how much greater becomes the meaning of the symbol when we see it as a direct descent from an operative practice! Our ancient brethren used the point within a circle as a test for the rectitude of the tools by which they squared their work and built their temporal buildings. In the Speculative sense we use it as a test for the rectitude of our intentions and our conduct, by which we square our actions with the square of virtue. They erected Cathedrals—we build the house not made with hands. Their point within a circle was operative—ours is Speculative.

But through the two—point in a circle on the ground by which an operative Master secretly tested the squares of his fellows—point within a circle as a symbol by which each of us may test, secretly, the square of his virtue by which he erects an Inner Temple to the Most High—both are Masonic, both are beautiful. The one we know is far more lovely that it is a direct descendant of an operative practice the use of which produced the good work, true work, square work of the Master Masons of the days that come not back.

Pass it not lightly. Regard it with the reverence it deserves, for surely it is one of the greatest teachings of Masonry, concealed within a symbol which is plain for any man to read so be it he has Masonry in his heart.

LODGE OF THE HOLY STS. JOHN

Dedication, solemnly setting apart for some sacred purpose, is a ceremony too ancient for its beginnings to be known. Just where Masons left off dedicating their lodges to King Solomon cannot be stated historically; traditionally, as the first Temple was dedicated to King Solomon and the Second Temple to

Zerubbabel, Masonry was first dedicated to Solomon, then to Zerubbabel, and finally, after Titus destroyed the Second Temple, to the Holy Sts. John.

But we do know that the dedication is very ancient; documentary evidence connects the name of St. John the Evangelist with Masonry as early as 1598. The connection must be far older; indeed, if we need further evidence of the possibility of the Comacine Masters having been the progenitors of the operative Freemasons we may find it in the frequent dedication of Comacine churches to one Saint John or the other. The whole island of Comacina is dedicated to St. John the Baptist and an annual festival and midsummer pageant are observed in his honor to this day.

St. John's Day in summer (June 24), and St. John's Day in winter (December 27) were adopted by the Church in the Third Century, after failure to win pagans from celebrating these two dates as the summer and winter solstices; that is, the beginning of summer and the beginning of winter. Not able to destroy the pagan festivals a wise diplomacy gave them new names and took them into the Church!

It was the custom for the Guilds of the Middle Ages to adopt saints as patrons and protectors, usually from some fancied relation to their trades. The operative Masons were but one among many Guilds which adopted one Saint John or the other; Masons adopted both as (explained in an old ritual), "One finished by his learning what the other began by his zeal, and thus drew a second line parallel to the former."

Whatever the reason and whenever the date, Free-

masons of to-day come from "the Lodge of the Holy
Sts. John of Jerusalem," meaning that we belong to
a lodge dedicated to those Saints, whose practices
and precepts, teachings and examples, are those all
Freemasons should try to follow.

THE PRINCIPAL TENETS

The Entered Apprentice receives a monitorial explanation of these which is both round and full, but
neither full nor round enough to instruct him wholly
in these three foundation stones of the Ancient Craft.
Nor can he receive that roundness and fullness of
explanation by words alone. He must progress
through the degrees, attend his lodge, see the Fraternity in action, fully to understand all that Freemasonry means by Brotherly Love, Relief, and
Truth.

But a word or two may clear away some possible
misapprehensions.

Brotherly Love is not a sentimental phrase. It is
an actuality. It means exactly what it says; the love
of one brother for another.

In the everyday world brothers love one another
for only one reason. Not for blood ties alone; we
have all known brothers who could not "get along"
together. Not because they should, not because it
is "the thing to do," but simply and only because
each acts like a brother.

Freemasonry has magic with which to touch the
hearts of men but no wizardry to make the selfish,
unselfish; the brutal, gentle; the coarse, fine; the bad,
good. Brotherly Love in Freemasonry exists only
for him who acts like a brother. It is as true in

Freemasonry as elsewhere that "to have friends, you must be one."

The Freemason who sees a Square and Compasses upon a coat and thinks, "There is a brother Mason, I wonder what he can do for me," is not acting like a brother. He who thinks, "I wonder if there is anything I can do for him," has learned the first principle of brotherhood.

"You get from Freemasonry just what you put into it" has been so often said that it has become trite— but it is as true now as when first uttered. One may draw checks upon a bank only when one has deposited funds. One may draw upon Brotherly Love only if one has Brotherly Love to give.

The Entered Apprentice is obligated in a lodge which wants him; all its members are predisposed in his favor. They will do all in their power to take him into the Mystic Circle. But the brethren cannot do it all; the Entered Apprentice must do his part.

Luckily for us all the Great Architect so made his children that when the heart is opened to pour out its treasures, it is also opened to receive.

The Entered Apprentice learns much of Relief; he will learn more if he goes farther. One small point he may muse upon with profit; these words he will often hear in connection with charity, "more especially a brother Mason."

St. Paul said (Galatians vi, 10), "As we have therefore opportunity, let us do good unto all men, especially unto them who are of the household of faith."

Freemasonry has no teachings that a Mason should not contribute to other charities. The continually insistent teaching of charity through all the three degrees, especially the Entered Apprentice's Degree, excludes from charity no one.

Without dependence societies, nations, families, congregations, could not be formed or exist. But the very solidity of the group, predicated upon mutual dependence, also creates this idea of distinction in relief or friendship or business as between those without and those within the group. This feeling is universal. The church gives gladly to all good works but most happily to relieve those "who are of the household of faith." Our government considers the welfare of its own nationals before that of the nationals of other governments. The head of a family will not deny his own children clothes to put a coat upon the back of the naked child of his neighbor. Those we know best, those closest, those united in the tightest bonds come first, the world over, in every form of union.

Naturally, then, a Mason is taught that while in theory for all, in practice charity is for "more especially a brother Mason."

The final design of Freemasonry is its third principal tenet—the imperial truth. In some aspects truth seems relative, because it is not complete. Then we see it as through a glass, darkly. But the ultimates of truth are immutable and eternal: the Fatherhood of God; the immortality of the soul.

As two aspects of the same object may seem different to different observers, so two aspects of truth may seem different. It is this we must remember when we ask, What is truth in Freemasonry? It is the essence of the symbolism which each man takes for himself, different as men are different, greater as perception and intelligence are greater, less as imagination and understanding are less. We are told, "On this theme we contemplate"—we think of the truths spread before us and understand and value them according to the quality of our thinking. Doubtless that is one reason for the universal appeal of Freemasonry; she is all things to her brethren and gives to all of us of her Truth in proportion to our ability to receive.

RÉSUMÉ

In the Entered Apprentice's Degree the initiate is taught the necessity of a belief in God; of charity toward all mankind, "more especially a brother Mason"; of secrecy; the meaning of brotherly love; the reasons for relief; the greatness of truth; the advantages of temperance; the value of fortitude; the part played in Masonic life by prudence, and the equality of strict justice.

He is charged to be reverent before God, to pray to Him for help, to venerate Him as the source of all that is good. He is exhorted to practice the Golden Rule and to avoid excesses of all kinds. He is admonished to be quiet and peaceable, not to countenance disloyalty and rebellion, to be true and just to government and country, to be cheerful under its laws. He is charged to come often to lodge but not to neglect his business, not to argue about Freemasonry with the ignorant but to learn Masonry from Masons, and once again to be secret. Finally he is urged to present only such candidates as he is sure will agree to all that he has agreed to.